For Those Who Don't Know Chocolate!

Amirah al Wassif

editor: Kris Haggblom
book design and layout: SpiNDec, Port Saint Lucie, FL
cover image: *The Tribe Must Choose*, by Kris Haggblom

Printed in the United States of America.

Published by Poetic Justice Books
Port Saint Lucie, Florida
www.poeticjusticebooks.com

ISBN: 978-1-950433-01-8

FIRST EDITION
10 9 8 7 6 5 4 3 2 1

For Those Who Don't Know Chocolate!

poetry by
Amirah al Wassif

table of contents

for those who don't know chocolate!

for those who don't know chocolate
the children of poverty
and the sleepers in the corners of ancient streets
for those who survive famines but are still hungry
for those boys who never dream
because they never sleep
for those who don't know chocolate
but only heard rumors about its sweetness
the people with half a soul
who lack food and live in imaginary houses

for those who crawl on the sharp platforms at
    midnight day after day
seeking the warmth to live
for those babies who have never tasted milk
who stare with wide eyes looking for any help
for the hands of charity
and the sensitive hearts which cry and bleed
for those who gather in the torn tents around the world
waiting such a long time
for those who don't know chocolate
and haven't the ability to imagine it

for the innocent faces washed by the rain
for the seekers of the smell of humanity in each dark alley
for those who kiss the sun through their contemplative
    glances
for those who write with heavy hearts and crushed dreams
the climbers of existence's shoulder
looking for the face of justice

for the dancers with bare feet on Everest's peak
who do their best to bring joy and peace
for the sun of tolerance warming our bones
for the bloom of the flowers
amidst the sky's gloom

for those who never tasted chocolate
but have heard about its magic
the crawlers of the earth with their great desire
to make the difference between the past and future

for those who draw in the sand
with belief in their friendship with the waves of the sea
for the people murdered in every battle
for the injured soldiers in every war
for those women who haven't the right to vote
for the mothers who have no voice

for the fishermen in their ships
for the highest star in our sky
and for the rainbow
for those people with disabilities
and for those players with woolen balls
for the little boys who sell water
for the little girls who feed the roosters

for the nations which suffer from drought
for the victims of racism
for the dead murdered by terrorism

a woman looking for a tongue!

they said your voice should not be heard
  we need a woman without sound
then I asked my god
o lord, do I count?
and he answered me in short
raise your voice and shout
they said we need a perfect doll
walking and stopping when we want
  but I am totally tweety bird
so, I whispered: no, I cannot
they said the good girl knows how to
close her mouth
she always pretends to ignore seeing
revolutions in the north
or in the south
  the good girl used to crawl
she must hide the bright side of her soul
good girl hasn't any right
or even fight for her vote
the good girl could not contemplate the faint light
in the middle of the road
they said we need a plastic woman
  but, I act like a real woman
  so, they cried "be shy"
but, I insisted to fly!

my arrogant silence

My arrogant silence looms over me
His voice like a truth
Like a bumble bee
My ears have the sight
Each ear has the right
To see!
It is such a messy heaven
Like taking a breath and given
The reality of to be
I am totally confused about that
Mixing good things and bad
Makes me as an island in the see
And while contemplating
My reality
I found, yes, I am that lonely island in the sea.

so lucky

so lucky because I am stuck here
in my kingdom, in my chamber!
carving my oddity alone
by the windows under the thunder
so lucky because I am struggling
like a fighter
eating my worries
create the adventure
feeling more than I should
thinking more than normal
so lucky because I am stuck here
laugh at my memories like a monster
imagining a big battle between me and me
hearing an imaginary whisper!
so lucky even though my body is covered
with the answer
of how all the beauty has been shortened
in the feather of a painter!
so lucky because I am not a member
when matter relates to a number
I am more than
I am the opener
of all locked doors
I am no border
and well
so lucky because I am a writer.

the poetry is

the poetry is the deep philosophy of the cry and laugh
it is the unseen language which touches our soul
  bitter and joyful

the poetry is the skin of the sensibility and the
  incredible race among the clouds
it is the pouring of the sky blue in our opening hearts

the poetry is the art of the mess
that far world which told you what lies behind the galaxy

it is our previous feelings and the forthcoming ones
when we believe in spirit and science and madness

the poetry is finding the details in eyes of another
it is this amazing ability to read the maps of souls
it is the smell of honey and the necessity of wings
and the tragedy of nights
it is long walking in the land of the imagination republic

the poetry is more than contemplating the moon
through a poetic night
it is more than rhythm and free verse
more than the extraordinary words and the visual scenes

the poetry is more than the silence of beauty
and the gossiping of people

it is what lies beyond breath
it is what lies beyond the sea
it is what lies beyond the legends

the poetry is discovering
  the hidden smile of the orphans!

windows of Madrid

I remember when we woke together in the ancient
    streets of Spain
when the fantastic windows whispered in my ears "hello"
I remember I felt a strong shiver which could heal any pain
I couldn't dare to reply
I thought that voice came from my fellow traveler
so I began to spy
here, I discovered the magnificent magic
her shape takes more than my like
when I jumped like a child in the street
because I fell in love with the windows of Madrid
this romantic story escaped from the old age
came to me and wrote its secret on my page
the beautiful windows of Madrid
inspired me to write in Casa María Plaza Mayor
it makes my soul sing for the coming light
for the healing of your suffering or pain
by the ancient art of Spain

a symphony!

between a finger and a finger
there is a flower
your love seems stranger
gives me the power
to act as a sea
to call you through me
even your name's letters
become a symphony!

traveling on the angel wing

traveling on the right wing of an angel
takes me away, away to my first dance
dragging ourselves through the fancy castle
shakes me today, today is my chance

oh! how far our starry night
oh! what a rare scare or fight
oh! the wonder of your face sight
oh! oh!

traveling on the right wing of an angel
reminded me how I did ride my horse
a supernatural scene, memory or dream
it was a fairytale, of course!

oh! how far our starry night
oh! what a rare scare or fight
oh! the wonder of your face sight
oh! oh!

traveling on the right wing of an angel
visiting the marvelous towns in his eyes
shouting like a child, a pleasure made circle
for walking in the land of the wise

oh! how far our starry night
oh! what a rare scare or fight
oh! the wonder of your face sight
oh! oh!

traveling on the right wing of an angel
led me to become a true crazy lover
your warmth in this night transfer simple
immediately heals all I suffer

oh! how far our starry night
oh! what a rare scare or fight
oh! the wonder of your face sight
oh! oh!

under the Sufi rain

under the Sufi rain, I am showering
there are higher voices that need to listen
while I am gorging my body with nature's leaves
the elder trees around me act the role of thieves
who steal your heart with magical fingers
and give you a rest
to lose your mind and become
a sinker in the wide forest!

the grass pray

once i wondered and started asking "why?"
why the mountain takes a strong role
without weakness, without death?
once i wondered and stood by
the green grass performing his prayers
glowing in a crazy sun ray
that had escaped his mother
and stayed here on the ground
illuminating the grass' prayer
catching the mountain's cry
while everyone sees a grim creature
the ray knows it is just a lie!

as an African child

As an African child
I crawled on mama's arm
Searching for an imaginary house
Which bears me with a fancy view
Of the coming clouds upon my head

As an African child
I jumped many times for seeing the clown
Who laughs and cries
Making jokes
Acts an excellent spy
With many children in their bed

As an African child
I saw the bitterness on mama's face
And tried to chase
Her shadow before her cheek was wet

As an African child
I drew my plan on the clay pot
I insisted to fly
Asking my sun to let
The charming of justice light
And asking the darkness to rest

at the funeral of 50 barefoot men

once upon a time
there was an ancient place
called Amon village
a very far spot
where everybody talks
about the river legend
a very far spot
where everybody knows
how to distinguish
the smell of fresh bread
there, at the Amon village
where all the folk live
in their dreams
and the blazing sun cries
against the face of heaven
there, where the poor sweeper
drowning in the colors of the rainbow
and the great brown mountains
announce their greatest secret
to the mass grave
in the Amon village
where everybody talks
about the river legend
and the tale of
50 barefoot men
in the ancient village
all people are storytellers
and all of them tell
the same story
which starts with

once upon a time
there were 100 men who
lived together in the same village
but 50 of them were barefoot
and the other 50 had fancy shoes!
50 men sweeping the streets
and 50 men making the bread
50 ones looking for more!
50 pairs of shoes in luxury leather
and 50 sets of toes inflamed and cracked

the river recognized the difference
between the shoes and the toes
then it made a good decision
according to nature's rules
and the river understood
the difference between
the torn clothing and the perfect ones
then it made a good decision
according to nature's rules

on the ragged edge, all the people walk
under the boiling sun
all people talk
and there were two kinds of talking
talking from shoe to shoe
and talking from toe to toe
and the river didn't love that kind of speech
so, it made a good decision

according to nature's rules

50 barefoot men carrying
their empty pots
their facial bones
tell you about long ages of bitterly
shabby dresses, fearful eyes
ancient faces full of pimples
much sweat
and shaky hands

50 barefoot men bearing their pain
looking for a way
to protect their feet
but the shattered glass
was everywhere

the dispossessed people died
and the rest were alive around the river
laughing, jumping, drinking
but the river has a sense of justice
so, it made a good decision
according to nature's rules
and, dried up!

greetings from the dark!

I remember! Yes, I remember this letter
When my tears decided to escape
I felt it was better
My soul took over my shape
I heard him laughing at me
   and clearly make fun
I could not understand how his love for me
Became hurtful like a gun

I remember! Yes, I remember this letter
When I fell to my knees
I remember your face in the paper
Looking smugly at me
The victim of a kidnapper
Or a tiny boat in a vast sea

I remember! Yes, I remember my love
Feeding my eyes your words
Your words, your shots!
Ah! I remember how I would
Keep it in my soul, my heart
But tell me how I could
Welcome your greetings from the dark?

as an extraordinary woman

As an extraordinary woman
I choose to fly
facing myself every moment
with no shame nor shy

as an extraordinary woman
I experienced more ways
adventuresome and dangerous
giving my sun new rays

as an extraordinary woman
I eat my worry
before it grows up
and makes me sorry

a courage woman boil the bananas

a courage woman boil the bananas
and watches her people on Haiti mountain
run away behind her dream
with curly hair and hidden pain
she bribes the sun with her smile
to dissolve the hot and murmured
"Amen"

a courage woman boil the bananas
and never experienced their taste
always surrounded with tents and hungrier
much secret there, in her chest
counting the footsteps in the sand
reveals how many persons are lost!

the Haiti girl plants the corn with her father on the
highest mountain
she ties his body with the ropes, she trying her best
and to make our life better
what should we do?
if we through our ages truly suffer
if all our times were blue?

a courage woman boil the bananas
and touches her baby skin
"Work...Work" a sound around cries in the space said
by men

she tore the tent with a huge passion
she never understands what is meant of station

where everybody needs to dream, to travel
but there is not her reality level

a courage woman boil the bananas
and watches her people on Haiti mountain
run away behind her dream
with curly hair and hidden pain
she bribes the sun with her smile
to dissolve the hot and murmured
"Amen"

a stranger

I am a stranger here and there
and nobody could end my fear
only that lonely cloud won't stop to stare
at me, every moment thinking of my affair
and I heard it cry from her spot there
"is everybody like my best friend there?
or is she the only case, mysterious and rare?"!

I love you despite what everyone knows!

I love you despite what everyone knows!
despite the traffic jams
despite the audience blame
and the chatter of my toes

I love you and I mean what I say
a confession of love accepts no delay
this type of the immortal love
cannot be temporary or tough

I love you despite the spread of boredom in the world
despite all my long nights, I was totally bent
I love you despite the breaking news and stammering
correspondence
I love you despite my classic shoes and the currency
of the tents

despite the urgent calls every midnight
I love you
despite the loneliness of shores after escaping the
light
I love you

despite the world difficult rules
despite the absence of "because"

I love you despite what everyone knows!

an urgent call in the second life

red rays of the unknown sun came down to my new window
a warm shiver touched me, made me laugh as a fresh baby
I decided to think about the source of these unknown rays
but, suddenly a kind of musical sound covered my ears
the sound did not seem like any earthly sound I had ever heard
it was a mix of waves and dancers and a creation of colorful birds
it was like a smell of honey and the secrets of gold

red rays of the unknown sun came down to my new window
fingers of nature throw fabulous jokes on my road
all the trees here like mothers, each tree gives me a kind hug
and I call them through songs of paradise
my songs are part of the skies
and my skies are all my world
in my second world, I do not have the time
to put my hand on my chest for wishing
all the clouds here are wishes
and I am a successful creature in hunting them with my glances

red rays of the unknown sun came down to my new window
fields of roses upon my head
rooms in the paradise full of supreme poetry
my soul thrilled at sewing the art of dream
and I am hungry for knocking on the door of memories
I know that nobody will respond
however, I insist on waiting
day after day
night after night
moment after moment

in my second world, I am walking on the roofs with bare feet
listening to the music makers in the tunnels of the heavens
here, we all are children of the upper world
and as a child, I am still awaiting
an urgent call in my new life

the motherland

When the motherland cries
Put your hand on your chest
For here, at this home lies
A doctor soul who does his best

When your motherland writes
Her best letter to your heart
Be touched by the words in nights
For her to create the perfect art

Of waiting till the moon speaks
And the crazy storm breaks
The glassy borders of your land
If she calls you now
Forget why and how
Just take this peaceful hand
And feel the smell of your motherland!

a question from the refugee camps

I asked them
How the sun says hello to everyone?
They laughed bitterly
Without being sorry
And told me "ask the gun"
Her red spark
Sharp like the dark
Permits entering the light for none

They asked me "what is the sun?"
When our expected meeting will be done?
Since their question
I did not ask again
Because everything was very clear
Through the war stain

There, in the Somali lands you can find the answers
Upon the clouds, in the camps, even on the children's
features
There, in the Somali lands all the details written with
no ink
The only truth here requires from you to think
About those people who do not have the fun
But you still ask about their sun?

Among the refugee camps in Baidoa
I found a baby that crawled
On the arm of his mama
Who, it seemed to me, frowned
The baby opened his eyes wide

Looking for the next light
But his mama knows
No light comes with fight

In a crowd of the lost African bodies
He holds my hand tenderly
He was selling water to the ladies
who were sitting on the docks
With their pots
Waiting for the day - early

In the Somali lands
They asked me
How the sun says hello to everyone?
I replied with no hesitation
No sun comes with a gun

people in the huts

People in the huts waving to me every day, every night
But the mental forces I have tell me that was not right
Beaming stones, a comfort zone, if I still am unbelievable
Midnight lies and the shortest of sight if I say it is reasonable
Oh! My brain! Could this daily scene
Be unreliable?

People in the huts waving to me every dark, every light
And my shocked eyes turn my thinking into a fight
Global channels, national banners talk regularly about me
Human battles, the press covers make a fairytale of me
Oh! My soul! Is this a fool
Dreaming what I see?

People in the huts waving to us every day, every night
Their clear truth is they're bigger than being on a diet
Sensibility drawing here their faces without quitting
And their words silently heard, emotions that need be written
Huts human certainly exist, every eye cannot be denied
Only these seeing them upset
The unfaithful eye or the blind!

lyrics dance

let the lyrics dare to dance
give the crystal moon a chance
clap your hands for your rapper with his fans

it is our time to grow
come to Everest and glow
all your gifts need to show

let the words dare to noise
tell the woman raise her voice
cry among the crowd of boys
"I am here"

give the chords more poise
make the music dissolve ice
stand by, announce your choice
everywhere!

let the lyrics dare to dance
give the crystal moon a chance
clap your hands for your rapper with his fans

Kafka decision

don't edit your soul according to fashion
it is not mine, it's a Kafka decision
get rid of their sayings, create your own vision
you're a free-whispered bird
and flying's your mission!

before my death!

before my death,
I would like to sit beside an innocent homeless girl
in front of one of the UNICEF banners
in our hungry wide street
talking together about the biscuits
and the magnificent toys and the ice cream

before my death,
I will try my best to make her
taste childhood's flavors
and she will try her best
to draw a false smile on her face
and because her cheeks will be
a mix of rosy and dirty
I will convince myself that
she is very happy!

before my death,
I would like to kiss all the flowers
especially the lilacs
I will be able to toss my grief aside
hoping to find a supernatural sign
one of those upper signs
which touches us gently
one of those upper signs
which take our souls for a long fabulous walk for free

before my death,
I would like to laugh in a loud tone
because I will be close enough to the political posters

which will hang everywhere
and I will sing one last song
for love and freedom
and I will dedicate it to the lonely and the frightened
and the immigrants and the dreamers

before my death,
I would like to toss
the most creative jokes
among the boys and girls
and I will gather the most delicious fruits
sending them to those who used to plant them
but never tasted any!

before my death,
I would like to kiss the famine babies wide-eyed
and saying "sorry" in another way
I will say it like a poem
escaped from the bottom of my heart
and appears of itself
in no-words

before my death,
I will praise the woman who works in breaking rocks
who fights in the day
and comes down in the night
an extraordinary woman knows how
to struggle under the angry sun
an extraordinary woman knows

how to fold her begotten's clothes
among the mess of rocks
an extraordinary woman knows
how to be a soldier in the battle
and a clown in the theatre at one time

before my death,
I will salute all the women
who work in breaking rocks
I will salute them with love and pity

before my death,
I would like to give
endless tickets
to the orphans around the world
and I will break my ego mirror
getting rid of my old grins
trying to find a true
smile similar to theirs

before my death,
I would like to share my food with a lost dog
in the corner of the road
or in the dirty narrow tavern

before my death,
I will learn how I must live!

far as the sky

far as the sky
close as a wish
we are all sailors
who never caught fish

far as the sky
close as a wish
we think of the questions
our poor and our rich

close as a wish
far as the sky
a day's role is to teach
life starts with "why"

close as a wish
far as the sky
great wisdom we reach
hello equals goodbye

far as the sky
close as a wish
the words we all cry
when we meet with death!

no intention to quit!

A kind of magic pumps in my chest
When the poetry lines weave their nest
More legends and tales spread along the mind
When the brilliant imagination ends his rest
My heart touches the honey light
Muse is manifest!
Take me slowly through the clouds
I am fevered from the reality mist
Tell me what the whole story's about
Give me a fast summary at least

A kind of magic pumps in my heart
When I'm lost in the garden or in art
More harmony overwhelms me
When my eyes meet the swart
Dance with me on the road
No matter shod or barefoot
Here we will witness our birth again
Let us absorb all the rain

A kind of magic pumps in my mind
More innovative horses need to ride
All the time in creating and
No intention to quit!

Amirah Al Wassif is a freelance writer based in Egypt. Her prolific output includes general interest articles, novels, short stories, songs, and of course, poetry. Five of her books have been written in Arabic and much of her English work has appeared in a great many cultural magazines. Her work has been translated into Spanish, Kurdish, Hindi and Arabic. Her children's book, *The Cocoa Boy and Other Stories*, illustrated by Sarah Hussein, will be published by Breaking Rules Publishing in 2019.

Grateful acknowledgement is made to the editors of the following publications in which Amirah Al Wassif's work has previously appeared:

Better Than Starbucks
The BeZine
The Bosphorus Review Of Books
Call and Response Journal
The Cannon's Mouth
Chiron Review
The Conclusion Magazine
Credo Spoir
Echoes Literary Magazine
Envision Arts
a gathering of tribes
Mediterranean Poetry Magazine
Merak Magazine
Otherwise Engaged - a literature and arts journal
Poetry Magazine
Praxis Magazine
Reach Poetry
spillwords
Street Light Press
Women of Strength / Strong Courage Magazine
The Writers' Newsletter
Writers Resist

CPSIA information can be obtained
at www.ICGtesting.com
Printed in the USA
LVHW110521060819
626642LV00001B/19/P